Sally and Chips Barber

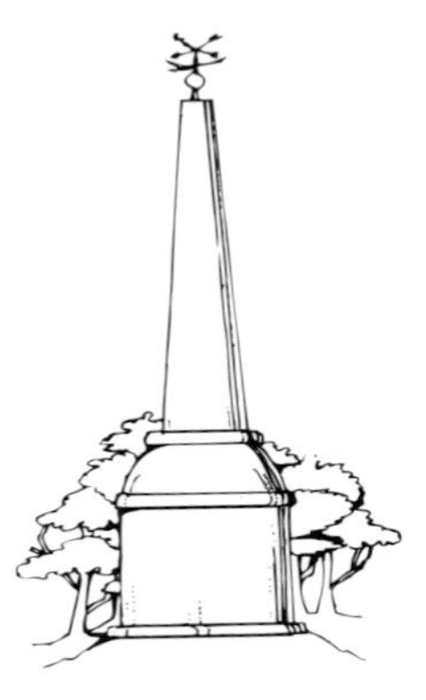

OBELISK PUBLICATIONS

Also by the Authors
Ten Family Walks on Dartmoor
Dark and Dastardly Dartmoor
Weird and Wonderful Dartmoor
Ten Family Walks in East Devon
Ghastly and Ghostly Devon
Haunted Pubs in Devon
The Ghosts of Exeter

Other Walking Books/Dartmoor Titles
Diary of a Dartmoor Walker, *Chips Barber*
Diary of a Devonshire Walker, *Chips Barber*
The Great Little Dartmoor Book, *Chips Barber*
The Great Little Chagford Book, *Chips Barber*
The Templer Way, *Derek Beavis*
Walks in the South Hams, *Brian Carter*
Walks in the Shadow of Dartmoor, *Dennis McCallum*
Walks in Tamar & Tavy Country, *Brian Carter*
Dartmoor Mountain Bike Guide, *Peter Barnes*
Colourful Dartmoor, *Chips Barber*
Cranmere Pool – the First Dartmoor Letterbox, *Chips Barber*
Pub Walks in the South Hams, *Brian Carter*
Walks in the Totnes Countryside, *Bob Mann*
Wheelchair Walks in Devon, *Lucinda Ruth Gardner*
Around and About Roborough Down, *Chips Barber*
Around and About Tavistock, *Chips Barber*
Around and About Lustleigh, *Chips Barber*
Circular Walks on Eastern Dartmoor, *Liz Jones*
Widecombe – A Visitor's Guide, *Chips Barber*
Dartmoor Letterboxing – A Guide for Beginners, *Kevin Weall*
The Dartmoor Quiz Book, *Chips Barber*
Along The Tavy, *Chips Barber*

Acknowledgements
All pictures by Chips Barber
apart from page 17 by Ken Leonard

First published in 1995, reprinted in 1996, 1998 and 2001 by
Obelisk Publications, 2 Church Hill, Pinhoe, Exeter, Devon
Designed by Chips and Sally Barber
Typeset by Sally Barber
Sketch maps redrawn from an out-of-copyright source by Sally Barber
Printed in Great Britain

Six Short Pub Walks on DARTMOOR

Introduction

These routes are for the many people who want only a short walk and prefer to avoid the bother of carrying huge rucksacks with all the paraphernalia that is associated with long treks in wild, remote country. Seasoned ramblers may think it is the soft option to resort to the sanctuary of an inn, perhaps with a roaring fire in the depths of winter, or a colourful beer garden at the height of summer. Far from it! The outings described in this little book are all very civilised affairs, particularly if you select, or are fortunate to have, decent days on which to do them.

We enjoyed all the routes and had bar snacks at each of the pubs. We didn't eat too much as we were in no hurry to rush headlong into the painful world of indigestion. We can assure you that we had excellent value and have no reason to believe that you won't either, but obviously menus can change and quality can fluctuate so we have shied away from specific detail. We did not choose these pubs for their food or drink but for the variety of walks that could be done to and from them – at Chagford we even leave the choice of inn to you, for there are four from which to choose!

If you want to clarify opening times or check on the range of meals on offer then we suggest that you ring beforehand to avoid any disappointment. The phone numbers have been included – but, again, they may change. Also, as pubs choose their own opening times, it's worth knowing in advance what these are, for there have been times when a pub has been approached, like an oasis in the desert, only to find the doors firmly shut for a few more hours!

As far as maps are concerned, the ones in this book are only simple sketch maps and we would strongly recommend that you carry the Dartmoor Outdoor Leisure map, Sheet 28, just one in a series specifically created for national parks and areas of outstanding landscape beauty. All the routes can be easily followed on that one sheet, but don't open it on a windy hilltop or you might find yourself flying above the scenery instead of walking on it! It is always wise to carry a compass as Dartmoor weather is so changeable – what starts as a lovely fine day can turn into something quite different!

We hope that you have as much pleasure following in our footsteps as we did in putting this book together. The whole experience of a pleasant ramble, a simple meal and a refreshing drink can be as good as any therapy. And, through the pages of this book, you perhaps might discover something of the history and heritage of the countryside that you pass through.

— Walk 1 —
In The Land of Devils and Angels
Dartmoor Inn, Merrivale
(about 2 miles)

The first part of this walk goes close to the Merrivale Firing Range so it is worth checking any firing times, or you may have a panic attack at the sight of red flags fluttering in the breeze from the prominent tors, should the military be in evidence. Details of firing for the week can be found in the local press on Fridays. Local police stations in the Dartmoor area will also have details. If you carefully stick to the route and do not wander too far in a general north-easterly direction, you will be all right.

There is a hill about 3 miles east of Tavistock, on the western shoulder of Dartmoor, called Pork Hill. The main road from Tavistock climbs it: first in a gentle manner, on the lower slopes of the hill, then with greater determination as it wends its way up onto the open moor. For many motorists the peak of this hill is far enough to go and the tremendous views, away to the west, from this lofty vantage point are well worth savouring. The popularity of the spot has led to a large, well-surfaced car park that is well patronised on fine days. There is no charge for such a privilege. Many who visit get no farther than the car park and seem content to get out their folding chairs and pass an hour or two on the adjacent open ground. It has almost become a local cliché, but it's shown in surveys that more than 90 per cent of those who visit the moor remain within a hundred yards of their vehicle. But you will be joining that almost elite band of adventurers who are prepared to work up a genuine thirst by walking a few miles first, which makes that first drink all the more rewarding.

If you park at the far (or Tavistock) end of the car park you will find a lovely relief sculpture to show the topography that presents itself in front of you, with information about places near and far. This fine instructional aid to the view was erected by the Royal Town Planning Institute to commemorate its seventieth anniversary and to contribute to the enjoyment of the countryside.

On this walk the Dartmoor Inn (01822 890340) at Merrivale is at about the half way stage, and you will need to be able to follow a map and straightforward instructions. A compass ought to be taken along, for even a general compass bearing to a road is

better than wandering unwittingly into the wilderness. These considerations are simply a case of being safe rather than sorry and the chances are that, like us, you will have a wonderful, problem-free walk.

Opposite the car park is a hill crowned by Cox Tor. Paths have been worn, but not too badly, through the vegetation, which lead to the top of the hill. Working on the assumption that you are at your fittest and freshest, then this is the time to tackle the hardest section of the walk. Gird up your loins and set forth up the hill towards the tor. Despite the upward trend, the terrain beneath your feet is fine for walking and it's possible to enjoy your surroundings safe in the knowledge that you are unlikely to be sent sprawling head over heels in an undignified fashion.

When you have just about gotten into your rhythm you will notice that the slope gets that little bit steeper. To your right are the remains of a small disused quarry. This side of the hill has bench-like slopes, which are the result of frost action, over a great period of time, on the altered slates and dolerites found here. Geologically the formations of Cox Tor are very different from the granite tors to the east of it.

When you scramble up the first obvious pile of rocks that confronts you, your euphoria at scaling them is immediately deflated by a realisation that it's another hundred yards to the top of the tor beyond this outcrop. A telltale trig. point is the place to get to, set amidst piles of rocks. From here the view is even better – Plymouth Sound visible with its 'book-ends' of Staddon Heights on the left and Penlee Point on the right. There are the hills and tors of the smaller and lower Bodmin Moor lying beyond that great depression of the Tamar Valley. To the north-west there is the triangular mass of Brent Tor, which is inextricably linked to Cox Tor by this legend…

There are several stories regarding the reason why a church was built in such an isolated but exposed location. One of them suggests that a wealthy merchant who was saved from drowning was so grateful to escape with his life that he had the church built on the first bit of high ground spotted from the sea. However, the Devil didn't like a church being built, so decided to disrupt proceedings by throwing down the building every time that it got started. The locals called for divine intervention; this arrived in the form of the Archangel St Michael, who, like your goodselves, stood atop Cox Tor. He selected a suitable projectile, a large boulder, and spying the Devil atop Brent Tor, beat all known records to throw the boulder to the distant rock. His accuracy was certainly to be applauded as the missile struck the Devil right between the horns. Nursing his headache, the Devil left the church builders alone and Brent Tor got its church.

In the knowledge that you have stood on the same spot as an archangel, you will be able to proceed across this heavenly moor. The next destination is the ridge of tors which lies a short distance away to the east, capped by some impressive piles of rocks. Roos Tor is the more northerly outcrop, to the left of the semipermanent pool in the depression ahead of you, and Great Staple Tor is the one on the brow of the hill to the right of it. This is the one to make for and can be easily reached by first walking down over the hundreds of mysterious little hummocks, almost like wavelets in the sea, to the small 'oasis', or pond, in the dip between Cox Tor and Great Staple Tor. A quick glance at the lie of the land will show that this depression is on the divide or watershed between the catchments that eventually feed either the River Walkham or the River Tavy.

The ground beyond the dip is rougher than anything so far and perhaps proof of the change of geology. Once attained, the highest piles of Great Staple Tor are a scrambler's paradise and, if treated with respect, provide those with boundless energy with a rocky playground in which to romp around. For those who like to indulge in a spot of letterboxing from time to time, there are several 'boxes' concealed in and around these granite masses. Those with less energy to burn can avail themselves of a seat on one of the many almost-comfortable flat granite rocks that litter this eminence.

Here, then, the route instructions may appear to be vague, so a look at the map might just reduce the amount of head-scratching and ease those furrowed brows. The aim is to get down off the tor and strike the main road just to the right of Merrivale's quarry. If you head well to the left of Middle Staple Tor and carefully pick your way over the clitter, which, we assure you, will soon become less of a rocky impediment to your progress, you will see the main road in the valley well below as it approaches Merrivale from the Princetown direction. You will also see the edge of the quarry. Head to the right of this. The more you descend the clearer it will be which way you should go. On reaching the road turn left and walk on the verge down to the Dartmoor Inn. It's one of the bigger and better Dartmoor hostelries and, like most pubs these days, serves a variety of meals.

The pub was once used for a live television discussion, hosted by Michael Buerk, on the subject of the military use of Dartmoor. In it farmers, preservationists, park officers, a politician and the military all aired their views on this emotive subject. Unfortunately there were technical problems and not all the arguments, for or against, could be heard by the viewers.

Many years ago there was a community of quarrymen living at Merrivale, many of them in the now long-departed terrace of cottages on the hillside above. The road has been improved here, leaving the one that runs by the pub as parking space.

Whilst you enjoy your pint, keep an ear or an eye out for any unusual noise that may emanate from upstairs. This is believed to be the spirit of a young Dartmoor maiden who lived and then died here, only to continue her ghostly wanderings along the corridors in the upper part of the pub.

All too soon it's time to leave. To get back onto the open moor it's necessary to walk back up the road for a short way. The second half of the walk is not as physically demanding as the first half but equally enjoyable. On the left hand side of the road, after about a hundred yards or so, a wall veers off to the left. Walk parallel with it. You may notice a small watercourse flowing along the hillside. This useful flow of water is the grand-sounding Grimstone and Sortridge. Not a building society, nor a brass band on tour from Yorkshire, this leat runs for many miles, built to carry a water supply to two ancient manors, those of Grimstone and Sortridge, near Horrabridge.

This leat soon leaves us to flow away to the right but we persevere onwards across this pleasant, easy-on-the-feet terrain, down towards a large rock ahead of us known as Vixen Tor. Stay with the wall until you are almost at the tor but do not attempt to walk a beeline to it. The tor is on private land but there is conditional access. Use the steps in the wall near a large rock just a bit farther on to the right. Provided that you have nimble, rather than clod-hopping, feet, getting over should be no problem. If you had one too many for the road at the Dartmoor Inn, then this can be your standard test for drunkenness.

This tor is more impressive from the other side and guide books often bill it as being the highest rock pile from summit to base. Located on the side of the hill, it gives a sphinx-like impression. The legend attached to it is featured in both *Dark & Dastardly Dartmoor* and *Diary of a Dartmoor Walker,* so we won't feature it here.

When you have explored the tor to your heart's delight, it is easier if you exit the same way and by the same four steps in the wall. Now turn left and keep the wall on your left hand side for several hundred yards. Avoid the temptation to cut straight across the small depression to Heckwood Tor. In between is a real mean mire that has had its share of victims. You have kept dry feet so far, so why buck the trend? All you have to do is follow the wall around and down to the point where it crosses a small stream beneath Heckwood Tor. You will also notice a stile that gives a different access into the compound where Vixen Tor is and by your astute powers of reasoning you will have deduced that you could have taken a short cut and exited here yourself. However, our route gave you a bit more exercise and was more foolproof in terms of reaching this point … honest, guv!

Having negotiated the stream, climb the hillside staying beside the wall. When you wish to regain your breath, stop, turn and look back at the view of the mightily impressive Vixen Tor and around to those other loftier tors that you have already climbed today. At the top, beside the track, are some enormous granite blocks that were probably cut here from the former quarry but remain in situ, possibly for all time. Leave the

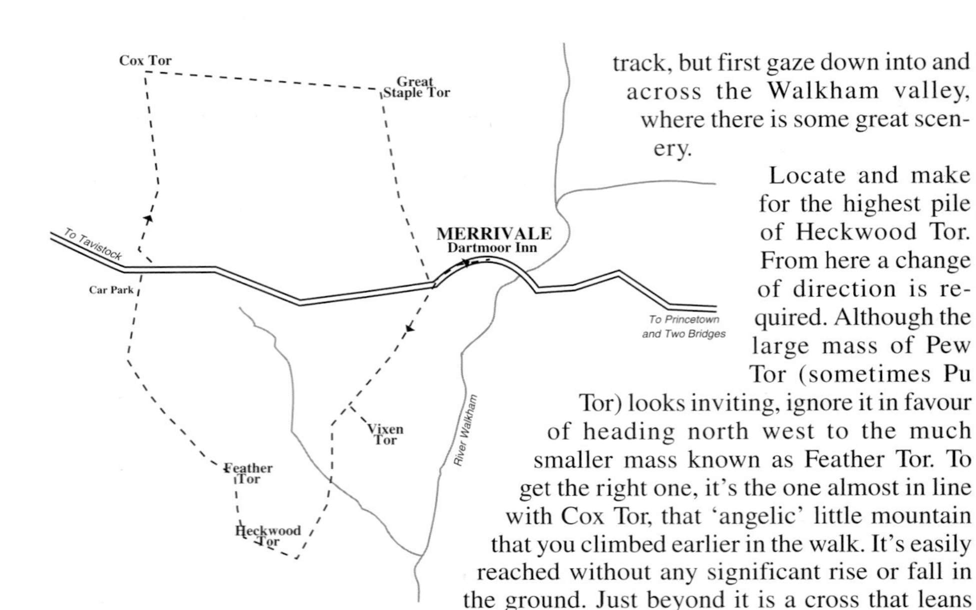

track, but first gaze down into and across the Walkham valley, where there is some great scenery.

Locate and make for the highest pile of Heckwood Tor. From here a change of direction is required. Although the large mass of Pew Tor (sometimes Pu Tor) looks inviting, ignore it in favour of heading north west to the much smaller mass known as Feather Tor. To get the right one, it's the one almost in line with Cox Tor, that 'angelic' little mountain that you climbed earlier in the walk. It's easily reached without any significant rise or fall in the ground. Just beyond it is a cross that leans like that of the famous tower in Pisa. This is Beckamoor Cross but is better known as Windy Post on account of the way the wind whistles past it. Definitely not a place to wear a kilt!

The Grimstone and Sortridge Leat is again encountered and we cross it to maintain a north-westerly course. By now you may be able to spy the outline of a track that runs over the western edge of Barn Hill, the slightly higher ground ahead of you. By getting onto this track and following it you will soon get back to the point from whence you set out.

— Walk 2 —
Stepping out in 'Stile'
Spoilt for choice!
(about 4½ miles)

There is a choice of four 'watering holes' – The Globe (01647 433485), Three Crowns (01647 433444), Buller's Arms (01647 432348), or Ring O'Bells (01647 432466).

This walk differs from most of the others in this book in a number of ways. If your main interest lies in the nature of the pub to be visited then you will be presented with a choice of several. If it's the walk that is of paramount importance then it's a walk with as many stiles as a steeplechase course has fences! It's a lovely walk designed to improve your blood circulation and get your heart pumping. (Yes, there is a steep hill along the way!) The real skill lies in your timing, for if it's a lunchtime pub call that you want you will need to allow about two hours of leisurely walking. If it's an evening visit it will depend on the time of year, as you will not want to be stumbling along in the dark – but do check the evening opening times!

The ancient stannary town of Chagford has a large free car park and it's here that you should park. It's located close to the parish church so head towards that and then look for signs. It's beside the library and health centre and village hall. Near the exit to the car park is a notice board that tells you something of the history of this moorland town. But if you want to know much more about its colourful past then we humbly commend The Great Little Chagford Book, *which, amongst much else, relates tales of the town's pubs.*

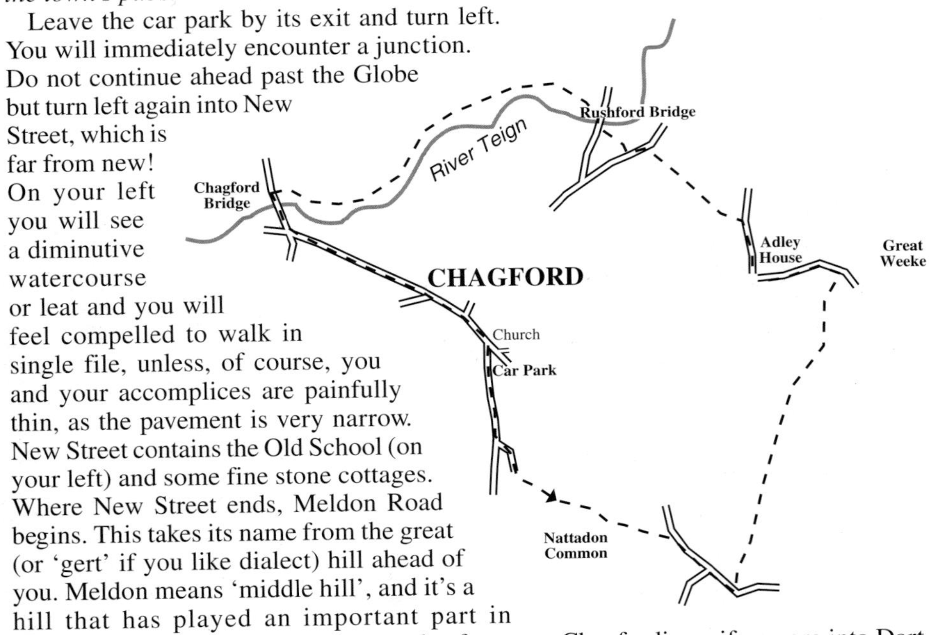

Leave the car park by its exit and turn left. You will immediately encounter a junction. Do not continue ahead past the Globe but turn left again into New Street, which is far from new! On your left you will see a diminutive watercourse or leat and you will feel compelled to walk in single file, unless, of course, you and your accomplices are painfully thin, as the pavement is very narrow. New Street contains the Old School (on your left) and some fine stone cottages. Where New Street ends, Meldon Road begins. This takes its name from the great (or 'gert' if you like dialect) hill ahead of you. Meldon means 'middle hill', and it's a hill that has played an important part in Chagford's past. It's still the back garden for many Chagfordians; if you are into Dartmoor letterboxing, there are many secreted within its various rock piles.

Today its undeniable delights are not for us, as Chagford's other hill of Nattadon awaits us. The good news is that it's not so high as Meldon; the bad news is that it is probably steeper! To get onto it, walk along Meldon Road until you see a green sign on your right opposite a turning on your left. This side road is called Nattadon Road, but the name plate is high up on the side elevation of the first house on the left of this rise. Turn left into this road and then bear right and proceed a short way along the road. A signposted green path to Nattadon Common, on the left, leads upwards. A gate is soon reached, where a small stream has to be crossed. Although there appears to be a choice of route, all paths lead up and over this little Chagford mountain. We headed straight across the stream if you want to follow our way precisely…

The mentality for including such a tough climb so early in a 'stroll' can almost be justified. If the end destination is a pub, you will have to work up a thirst, and if there has to be a tough bit, surely it's better to do it when you are freshest! Just take this hill in easy stages – pause at regular intervals to enjoy the ever-increasing panorama. There is even a strategically located bench, if you want home comforts for a brief respite.

There is no need to go over the summit of Nattadon; the obvious path climbs over the hill's left shoulder. Ahead you may see a wall with a barbed-wire fence coming in from your left. As you ascend the hill, without oxygen, you will see it closing in. Where you reach it the gradient starts to become more benign. Below you is rooftop Chagford and away towards the higher moors of Northern Dartmoor are many landmarks, like the giant dome-shaped Cawsand Hill (locals call it Cosdon), or the apparently flat-topped granite rock of Kes Tor. There are many fine paths and walks to be had in the area between the high open moors and Chagford. If the climb took its toll, take heart, for the rest of the walk is a 'doddle'!

Walk parallel with the hedge. To your left the land falls away for hundreds of feet.

This is where the Teign has carved a deep depression known as the Teign Gorge. Castle Drogo sits sentinel on the hillside as if guarding its entrance. Ahead of you are some plateau-like commons, the highest one being Mardon Down above Moretonhampstead. To the right of this you may just be able to discern another lonely rock pile. This is Blackingstone Rock near Doccombe. This tor is snugly surrounded in fields and forests. It has the luxury of possessing a ladder to help you attain its summit.

Continue until you reach a grassy car park. If the question crosses your mind, "Why didn't we park here to start the walk?" ask yourself whether you are glad the climb is over and done with!

Go straight across the car park and exit onto the road to the right. The road is a quiet lane and you are not staying on it for very long. There is a junction to the right, which we will ignore, pointing to Weddicott. This is a general direction; it fails to differentiate between Higher and Lower Weddicott. The 1:25000 Leisure Map shows both in their full glory.

At the next bend there are paths leading away from the road on the left side of the road. The one we want is the public bridlepath that goes downhill towards Great Weeke and Yellam. It's worth noting that this common is Week Down but the hamlet at the foot of its northern side has an extra 'e'. Perhaps you might like to look for the missing letter as you head down from the down! The path is well defined and soon leaves the open common to pass through an avenue of trees.

The way ahead is simply a case of downhill stuff, taking any obstacles in your stride – even the gates are not of the type that require a university degree in engineering to open them. You will eventually reach a crossroads of signposted paths, but opting for the straight-on approach should see you hurtling onwards without any problems of navigation at this juncture. The track soon gets steeper downwards and bears all the telltale hallmarks (or is it hoofmarks?) of an ancient sunken cattle drove route. The track, deep beneath high hedges, would have enabled cattle or sheep to be removed from Week Down with a minimum of supervision, just like your goodselves were!

The only drawback of such a fine corridor is that it lacks the views that other parts of the walk enjoy. On reaching the road at the bottom, turn left. After about 300 yards you will reach a junction where there is a letterbox and you will, no doubt, curse if you have a number of parcels in your rucksack that you were intending to post here and discover that it will only accept letters. Drat!

You will also notice, using your astute powers of observation, that if you maintained the straight course ahead you would be in Chagford in just half a mile. Sorry, we are not going that way. Turn right into Adley Lane – all the best bits of the walk are still to come.

Not far along this lane is a modern bungalow on the right with three trees opposite it. Just beyond is a half-hidden signpost on the right that points to the left along a short track. Follow this to the point where you are informed that this is private land and that you are requested to stay on the straight and narrow path and to keep your dogs under control. The way across the field is a delightful diagonal one and if you enjoyed that then the way across the next one continues the trend. Civilisation now rears its head as the way ahead is along a thin path, complete with Neighbourhood Watch, between dwellings and into a cul-de-sac in outer Chagford! Continue straight on and in a matter of yards another road will be reached. Turn left and you will see, this time on your right, a signposted path to Rushford Bridge. Cross the obligatory stile and make sure that you do not thump your high-precision, delicate camera against the stoneware there!

This field is a slight dogleg to the left as Rushford Bridge, spanning the River Teign, soon shyly presents itself nestling among some verdant splendour (surrounded by trees).

Cross the bridge and you will immediately spot a footpath leading off to the left across the level grassy meadows beside the river. Note that you will not be permitted to cycle as you pass this way, once you have skipped over yet another stile.

About one hundred yards along this grassy corridor you will have something of a choice and you need to make your mind up now whether you trust your sense of balance. Consider this choice at the first large isolated tree, just to the right of the path where it passes the end of a hedge on the left.

If you dislike the notion of balancing across a clam (a bridge made out of a fallen tree) that spans a small leat several hundred yards ahead, an obstacle that suits those who are fleet-of-foot, take the first easy option. However, if you have a gladiatorial approach to walking and enjoy the threat of possibly being pitched headlong into a watery ditch then take the second option. Those who take the second may well wonder what all the fuss was about…

The first easy option is to look to your right at this point, where there is a gap in the hedge at a small depression. Pass through it, but immediately bear left behind the hedge to a small wooden bridge over a leat just yards away. Proceed across that and follow the path. Soon a choice of routes is offered. Follow the direction to Chagford Bridge. The well-worn path is part of the official Two Moors Way that begins (or ends!) at Ivybridge and traverses Dartmoor, the mid-Devon plain and Exmoor to reach the Bristol Channel coast at Lynmouth. This section runs along the bottom of the fields, staying parallel with the leat, which originates from a weir that you will soon reach by persevering with this pleasant path.

The second option delivers you to the same weir. However, the route is through the fields, beneath the trees, to the inclined tree that affords a potentially safe passage over the leat near its start by the weir.

The best bit of the whole walk is from this weir up to Chagford Bridge. The river has that lovely wine colour, matured on the moor and vintage by the time it trundles past these fern-filled meadows. The path stays close to the Teign as it wends its way gently along to the ancient but very solid granite structure of Chagford Bridge.

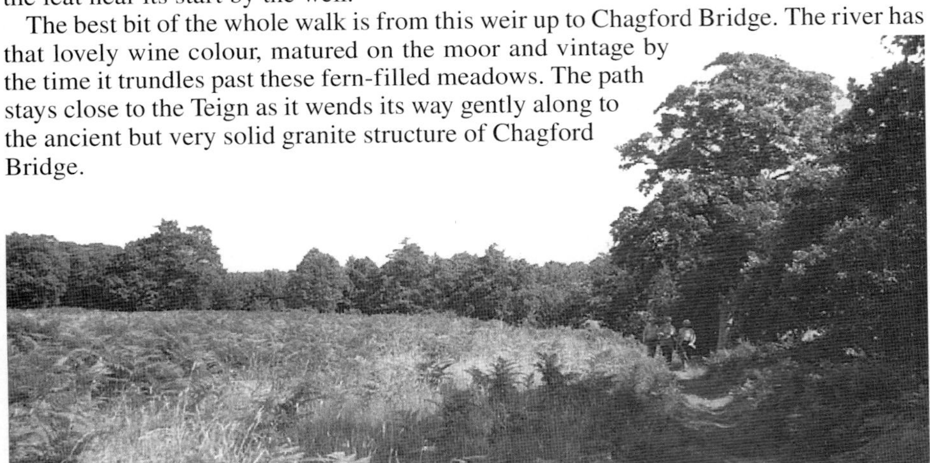

Emerging onto the road, turn left to cross the bridge and walk up the road to the junction. This time you are allowed to avail yourself of the turning, left to Chagford. Just follow the road up the hill and through a cutting in the bare rock. Although it's a steepish incline, the knowledge that it's the end of the walk, with a plethora of pubs from which to choose, is a sufficient spur to make your attempt at this very last hill one accomplished with a spring of step. The first pub you get to is the Buller's Arms, but for good measure there are also the Ring O'Bells, the Three Crowns and the Globe, all in a direct line on the route back to the car park … Can't be bad, can it?

— Walk 3 —
Something Beginning with 'H'
Forest Inn, Hexworthy
(about 5 miles)

Hexworthy and Huccaby are two small hamlets beside the West Dart River just before it summons up the strength to carry around one more great curve to join its partner, the East Dart River, at the appropriately named Dartmeet. Hexworthy is on the west bank and Huccaby on the east. This stroll combines the two separated by the watery divide but, as nothing in life is ever that straightforward, this walk takes an indirect route to get from one to t'other!

The starting point is at the pub, this time the Forest Inn (01364 631211) at Hexworthy. If you park just up the hill from the inn, it will lessen the initial ascent that you have to make, for this walk starts by walking up the twisting road to the brow of the hill, marked with a junction and a choice of routes.

If the weather, in the days leading up to your excursion, has been very wet, then it may be inadvisable, perhaps even impossible, to cross the West Dart River. In such a circumstance, when you reach the road near Combestone Tor, turn left and follow it back to the Forest Inn, thereby shortening the walk to 4 miles.

Our first manoeuvre is to turn right towards Sherberton, which is shown as being some three-quarters of a mile away. But we are not going to stay on this surfaced road for too long – it's only being used until access is possible to the open moor. Various gates on the left, and an intimidating barbed-wire fence, are ample evidence that these rough pastures or enclosures are private lands. However, a few hundred yards along the level road, on the left, salvation is at hand in the shape of a public bridlepath, complete with its blue dot. This short path leads to a gate where, in the lambing season, a sign reminds those who are being taken for a walk by their dog that they should take care to keep their canines on a lead and under great control. Go through the gate to the open moor, but do not follow the track that leads off to the right. This travels up the valley of the Swincombe, a tributary river of the West Dart that was the subject of much controversy some years ago. The Dartmoor Preservation Association staved off, after a long-drawn-out battle, the authorities who wanted to build a reservoir there.

Our way is simple, as a wall on the left is all that needs to be followed. Keep it to your left as you gently climb the lower slopes of Down Ridge. Almost immediately you will cross a dry leat, one of many that you will encounter on this walk. The wall changes direction and so must you. Follow it around to the left. Parallel to it you will see a path of sorts, which will peter out but will give you your direction. The views of Dartmoor from this hill are wonderful. Behind you are the Hessary Tors: North with its television mast and South with its elevated rock pile. To your north is the area that some folk 'in the know' refer to as the great Central Basin, a depression between the high Northern Moors and the slightly less high Southern Moor. In between, the East and West Darts run through a marginally less elevated area that includes Two Bridges and Postbridge. Several plantations can be spied, with tors peaking above and around them. This is probably the most strikingly beautiful part of the moor, as there is such a rich diversity of landscape – Dartmoor at its very best! If you want landmarks, look out for the great Yar Tor, dwarfing the cars crawling ant-like towards it up the steep Dartmeet Hill. Warren House glistens in the morning sunlight, whilst Hameldown's bulky ridge is always an impressive sight. However, it's more fun to get out your map and identify them yourself. Laughter Tor should keep you amused!

After about half a mile of walking along the contour of this hill you will see a green path emerging from the enclosures on the left. This is the one we want to follow upwards over the moor. It's a splendid track, not too tough on the feet, that curves and rises gracefully up and around the south-eastern edge of Down Ridge. A repaired cross stands to the left of the track, and if you want to take a coffee break, out of the wind, a small disused mine working a few yards below it is a pleasant venue.

The track continues up towards the old mine workings of Henroost. We did this walk in August; the track and the surrounding vegetation, a riot of yellow and purple moorlands, were very similar to the North Yorkshire Moors. At some ruins, beside the track on the right, continue onwards retaining the same course. A short distance farther on a T-junction of routes is met, complete with a seven-clapper span over the tiny stream. Don't turn right up the slope to the Henroost, as named on the map, but turn left onto the track that runs across the hillside beneath the disused Hooten Wheals, yet another place beginning with an 'H' in a day dominated by this letter. This track has some foul mires beside it, so don't stray from it.

To see the ruins and disused gullies today it's hard to imagine this idyllic setting is where men grafted hard and long, often in horrendous working conditions, to produce top-quality tin ore. The leats that are so numerous around these hillsides provided the necessary power to drive the machinery. Tin mining was a sporadic activity and, although these mines enjoyed a renaissance in the 1890s and another just before the First World War, it wasn't many years before they ceased production for all time. However, the industrial archaeologist can literally have a real field day piecing together how these mines, the grand-sounding Hooten Wheals and Henroost Mines (Hexworthy Mine), may have operated or been operated. Some of the buildings have decayed through neglect, but Americans based in the vicinity during the Second World War hastened their demise by using them for target practice!

The track runs out at the point where the stamps and dressing floors are visible. So far you have had it fairly easy, with little to go wrong in following the directions, but now you will have either to pay close attention – in order to follow in our footsteps – or to improvise your own way for the next mile or so. Given clear conditions, this should be no more than a little demanding, but in the mist you may need to use your compass

wisely. If the dreaded were to occur – a thick mist and *no* compass – a general downhill course through any intervening wetland would at least see you ultimately down to Saddle Bridge, where the O Brook reaches the road from Holne (another H!) to Hexworthy.

The general idea of this part of the walk has been to work around the higher parts of the O Brook keeping near one level, at least for a while, so as not to have to drop down the hillside and then climb up again. In trying to achieve this highland loop the following route instructions may prove useful.

From the industrial remains just mentioned, look across the hillside in a projected line ahead, on a similar level. A tree may be spotted ahead. To the right of it is a grassy area below rougher vegetation. Follow the dry leat around this slope. However, a stream and its accompanying marsh have to be crossed first. This is no problem, as long as you don't weigh two tons and are not wearing stilettos! Beyond the tree is another, higher up the slope – you will head just left of this. But another little depression, complete with resident stream, will temper your haste over this edge of what might be described as the outer limits of Holne Moor. The going underfoot is not as good, squelchier than we have been used to today and wetter than we'd like. However, when you have struggled gamefully to a point just above two trees, some fifty yards down the hillside, Combestone Tor will be seen, invariably with cars in the car park right beside it. It's all right to veer just right of this pair of somewhat stunted specimens, to head now down the hillside to the stream at the bottom – Dry Lake – just a short distance from where it joins the O Brook. A path,

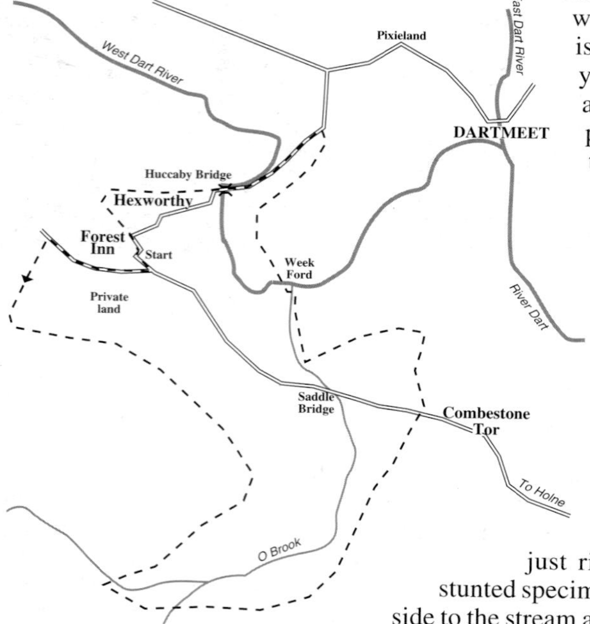

of sorts, rises up the shoulder of the hill through the ferns and then maintains a parallel course with the O Brook towards Combestone. It is not necessary to visit the tor, so head just left of it, keeping well up the hillside, over the remains of two walls running down the slope. Eventually a dry leat, complete with an occasional bridge over it, will be seen ahead and going conveniently in your direction. Follow it, walking in its bed as this is the better terrain, to the road just below the tor. The leat continues beyond the road but here you cannot walk in it so 'delete' that option and walk beside it until you meet an obvious track going on down the hill. This stony track makes a beeline for Dartmeet. However, this is not our destination and when we have crossed a cattle grid, at 'Combestone', some way ahead, surrounded by a veritable orgy of granite dry-stone walling, we see a signpost that gives a change of direction.

The way now lies along the bridlepath to the stepping stones at Week Ford. But that's easier said than done! Ignore any public right of way shown on the Outdoor Leisure Map – it certainly isn't there on the ground. If you see the way the sign points you will notice that there is a gully to your right and a stout stone wall to your left. Head downhill, between the two, crossing a line of boulders not far from the signpost. At the bottom of this enclosure is a gate on your left. Beyond it you will see a fork in the paths. Go through the gate and take the right fork which is a grassy corridor that leads over a low hill before passing through a gap in the wall. It's a pleasant romp down into the valley where the O Brook is audible, but not visible, as it rushes down its tree-lined course to join the West Dart at Week Ford. It lies beyond a barbed-wire fence. Turn right and follow the fence. Don't let it out of your sight and you will reach the next destination. This leads to a small footbridge to cross the O Brook on your left. Use the right-hand handrail as the left hasn't got one! To cross the West Dart it's a case of how long your stride is when it comes to stepping over the 'man-made' blocks of granite, of which there are about 18 or so. One small step for Man is not enough!

The relief of having crossed this major obstacle is slightly diminished by the normal state of the first section of the path that leads us on to Huccaby. Horses are heavy creatures and the narrow path is soft. The combination has caused a deeply muddy channel that is best suited to the fleet-of-foot, who can dance their way through the mire picking out the more solid spots.

The path soon becomes drier but only at the cost of a steady upward climb between moss-covered granite stone walls. At the top is a rustic footpath sign, hardly in pristine condition. It tells us that we have just come along a 'path' and that if we maintain our course we shall continue along a 'path'. That information gleefully stored in the memory banks, continue on to a point, with stereo signs, where a path comes in from the right. Keep straight ahead downhill to a gate that you will have to pass through. There is one of those lovely ambiguous signs here: 'Cattle please shut this gate'. We dallied a while but no cow performed this deed whilst we were watching!

Go down to the nearby road and turn to the left. Take care, as this road leads to the popular beauty spot of Huccaby (also known as Hexworthy) Bridge, where people like to congregate in large numbers on high days and holidays. Stroll past the Chapel of St Raphael, built on the site of some former cottages, with its chapel chimney, the fire keeping worshippers warm on wild winter days in the past. A large hearth used to boast a peat fire that smouldered away through the services there, as a concession to the harsh Dartmoor winter climate. It was, no doubt, an encouragement to entice parishioners to come to church, as it would have been an austere experience without some warmth. It also doubled as a day school for the local moorland children and was originally thatched with rye straw.

Beside you, beyond the trees, the West Dart is now seen, higher upstream than when you first crossed it at Week Ford. And you have to cross it again at Huccaby Bridge, which you will reach quite soon. On busy days you will be able to see motorists approach it from opposing sides, blind from each other. Narrow Dartmoor bridges are barometers of human tolerance levels and it is not unusual for irate motorists to become more overheated than their vehicles! Fortunately pedestrians can nip over smartly and avoid any confrontation of this type.

Immediately beyond the bridge, on the right side, is a footpath that you will get onto once you have scaled the wall. To facilitate your passage, stone steps have been introduced, but beware of a loose one on top. We tried paths daubed in blue markers; now it's time for a preponderance of yellow markers. The way ahead is straightforward, with a few more obstacles to encounter in these fields. Below to your left is the back of Jolly Lane Cot, the last house remaining in England to be built in a day in order to claim squatters' rights. It was built by Tom and Sally Satterley and friends on midsummer day in about 1832. They had to have smoke coming out of the chimney before the sun went down to claim their home and land rights. This they did whilst the local gentry were away, blissfully unaware, celebrating at a local fair.

It's about time we were celebrating too, so on reaching the various gates of a farm, pass through each one, remembering to close them, until you reach an attractive thatched cottage. Turn left here and follow the lane all the way, just a few hundred yards, to the pub!

The Forest Inn was originally a thatched inn but a fire virtually destroyed it in 1913. The bulk of the building that you see today was built in 1916 beside and incorporating the first inn. However, some years later this was replaced by a larger extension. For those who know and love Dartmoor it's good to be at a place where Dartmoor's greatest writer, William Crossing, who died in 1928, spent many happy nights. For a number of years Dartmoor 'letterboxers' regularly met here at the seasonal changing of the clocks, in March and October, to exchange letterbox stamps, secrets and stories. They now meet at Princetown.

Hopefully now you will be a little more familiar about these places that begin with an 'H'. Certainly most reference books about Devon written on an A–Z format don't even mention Huccaby or Hexworthy – shame on them!

— Walk 4 —

Life's Little Ups and Downs!

Dartmoor Inn, Lydford

(about 2 miles)

Not one but two Dartmoor Inns in one book! You will have to decide the timing for yourself but this short walk of about two miles might take longer than you expect, as there is one climb to slow you down.

This Dartmoor Inn (01822 820221) is on the main road, the A386, between Okehampton and Tavistock, about halfway between these two towns. Just yards before it on the Okehampton side of the inn is a narrow, rough lane that passes through a gate, Moorgate, to an open down and a public, purpose-built car park. Park here. In the past locals, who knew this spot, would drive on over the down to the River Lyd, but this proved a visual eyesore and to reduce damage to the down this less obtrusive and intrusive car park was made. Now, without the vehicular invasion over High Down, it's a more pleasant haven: what Dartmoor should be like! The walk stays outside the Willsworthy and Okehampton firing ranges, but if the military are active you will see red flags flying from some of the higher peaks.

Almost immediately a gate is passed through and about 80 yards farther on is a bench, balanced on two granite stones. On it there are these words: 'In memory of a special son, Stuart Thayre (1951–1986). Until we meet again may God hold you in the hollow of his hand.' This is the first of several memorials that lie along the way.

Just a few yards beyond, there are stone steps strategically placed in the wall to make your passage over it a much easier one than it would be without them.

Now if you haven't been here before, and if the weather is sunny and pleasant, you will be impressed by the beauty of the scenery, with the steep north-western slopes of the moor rolling down, from great heights, towards you. The hills are capped by some stunning tors: the one with a cross is Brat Tor, and the one to the left of that, on a similar level, is Arms Tor.

On your left is a wall, a very long one known as the King Wall, which runs beside a once-important route, the King Way. Until 1817 the line of this was the main road from Tavistock to Okehampton.

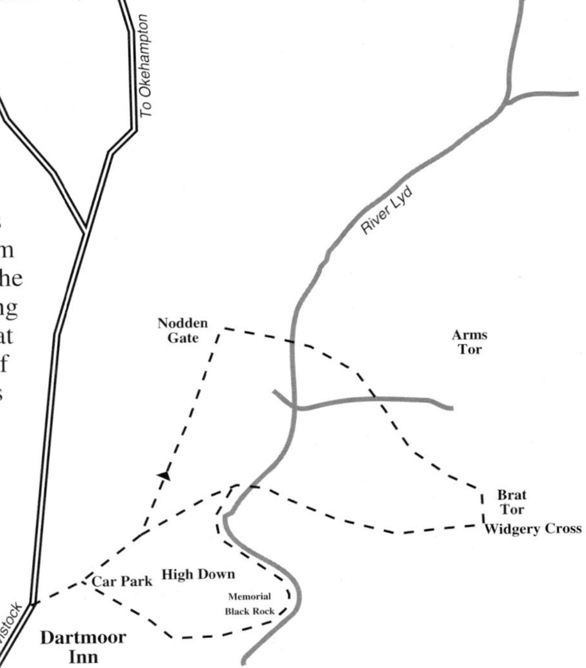

Keep the wall to your left until, after about a quarter of a mile, you reach Nodden Gate. Ahead is the most peculiarly shaped hill on Dartmoor. Great Nodden is a gigantic bulge, with an east face as steep as almost anything found on the moor. Fortunately we are only to glimpse it in the distance as we turn sharp right to follow a stony track for about 100 yards. It bends off to the left whilst we stay with the line of the hedge, now on our right, to go downhill to a ford over the Lyd. It's a little hard to imagine that this is the same brook that sometimes is such an impressive torrent gushing wildly down through Lydford Gorge, a few miles downstream. There are no Devil's Cauldrons up here!

To cross the moorland Lyd you are blessed with a choice: stepping stones just to the right of the bottom of where the wall comes down to the stream or, slightly farther upstream – a matter of yards – is a fording place, ideal for a hot day when you are not concerned about an occasional 'British Standard Bootful' of water.

Beyond, through the ferns, is a grassy path that climbs the hill between Arms Tor, on your left, and Brat Tor, on your right. The object is to climb to the top of the cross-bearing Brat Tor. Inevitably this climb of about 400 feet will be the toughest part of this short excursion. Follow this grassy corridor that gives you a gentle start to the ascent. The track crosses a tiny stream. As soon as you have crossed it, it's better to veer to the left of your destination. There are gully-like depressions higher up the hillside to your left. If you skirt the right-hand edge you will avoid some potentially wet, marshy ground. Soon you will reach a very obvious track coming down the hillside at an angle to you. The least painful or breathless way to reach the top of the tor is to turn left onto this track (which runs up to the disused peatworks at Rattlebrook) and follow it up the hill for a few hundred yards. Using your powers of judgment you will soon see a path, of sorts, leading right and up to Widgery Cross on Brat Tor.

Although there are higher tors in this district, you will still get that euphoric feeling of being on top of the world, with the most wondrous of views set out before your very eyes. The panorama embraces such high spots as Brent Tor, with the distant heights of Bodmin Moor away to the right of that. The far horizons stretch along the north Cornish coast, near Boscastle, around and past Bude and up into North Devon towards Hartland Point. In between, in the great rolling landscape to the north west of this tor, are numerous small villages, many of them on breezy hilltops, others secreted in deep valleys of rivers with unfamiliar names – the Lew, Thrushel, Waldon, Neet, Claw, Carey and Deer being just some of them. The surrounding tors also form a pleasant prospect from here, with the impressive Great Links Tor, complete with shoulder-high trig point, stealing the show. Hare Tor, Sharp Tor and Chat Tor cap the high ridge less than a mile away. At a lower elevation Doe

Tor is visible, with the Doe Tor Brook tinkling merrily down beneath it to pass the ruins of Doe Tor Farm before reaching its confluence with the Lyd.

The cross, standing proud at about thirteen feet tall, is probably far bigger than you expected to find. It is named Widgery Cross after William Widgery, who was responsible for it being there. It commemorates the Golden Jubilee of Queen Victoria, celebrated in 1887. The tor has been called Bra Tor, possibly because it sits abreast the hill, and also Widgery Tor after the man and his commemorative cross. The Ordnance Survey records it as Brat Tor, but the spelling of this (and numerous other Dartmoor names) has fuelled arguments, with many very knowledgeable folk refusing to accept modern spelling changes.

William and his son, F. J. Widgery, were both talented artists and their landscape paintings are highly regarded. F. J. Widgery had his Christian name initials adopted by the City of Exeter for its car registration letters.

Now that you have recovered, perhaps having first scurried around looking for a letterbox or two, had a drink or a nibble, or simply enjoyed the view, your restless spirit determines that it's time to go. You have had a little more added to your Dartmoor education so it's socially acceptable for you to head back to your car or the pub or both! The way ahead is downhill, to the ford over the Lyd that you can see hundreds of feet below. The first section is steep; so steep, in fact, that one of our party had no sooner uttered a warning of the potential slipperiness when he entertainingly (albeit unintentionally) demonstrated the fact by trying to overtake on the inside at ground level! However, all you have to do is to take care that the grips on your footwear are sufficient to keep you in total control of your downward destiny.

The track reaches a footbridge, with a right-hand handrail, over the Lyd. As an alternative, to the left there are some stepping stones, which are not as convincing as they were some years ago.

If you have more energy to burn, and time at your disposal, there is a potential short diversion. About 300 yards downstream, on the west bank of the river, is a bench and another memorial at Black Rock, this time to Captain Nigel Duncan Ratcliffe Hunter. He wrote a poem here, at the time of the First World War, comparing a Dartmoor river to life itself. Shortly afterwards he was killed in action. The details on the plaque reveal

the love of the moor felt by this young man and the spot where it's located is, appropriately, one of the loveliest on Dartmoor. A nearby waterfall completes the beauty of the scene. If this detour is taken, a track leads from Black Rock back over High Down to the end of the walk.

Those whose weary bones can stand no more tormenting, once they have crossed the Lyd, simply have to keep the wall, stretching away from the river, on the right until the end is reached.

When you visit this Dartmoor Inn keep an ear and eye out for the various ghosts that haunt this ancient inn. It's not unknown for beer glasses to lift, without any human help, off their hooks and remain airborne for seconds until they come crashing down. Spooky! It's just one of many stories featured in our book *Haunted Pubs in Devon*.

— Walk 5 —
A Quick Dart to the Pub!
Tavistock Inn, Poundsgate
(about 3 miles)

New Bridge is very old! In fact almost anything in Devon that is called 'new' is probably quite ancient. It is a stone bridge on the road that runs from the A38 at Ashburton across the moor to Dartmeet. The road is a twisting, tortuous one and at times can be a test for raw nerves as there are always those who like to exhibit their prowess by driving along it at speed. The first bridge out from Ashburton, on an awkward chicane, is Holne Bridge. New Bridge is up and over the next immense wooded hill, a few miles farther on. A large car park is sited on the west side of the bridge, as are the toilets. Other facilities are there in the summer, including the all-important ice cream van that helps revive the flagging spirits at the end of an energetic stroll.

The River Dart flows strongly through its valley here, having carved a mighty chasm in the country in this district. A look at the map reveals that this lovely river has a real problem in finding its way to the sea. From Sharrah Pool (697717) to Holne Bridge it shows shades of the even mightier Mississippi. Between these two points a sober crow would need to fly just a tad more than 2 miles, but a salmon would have to swim more than two and a half times as far – 5 miles! As we make our way, especially to higher ground, we will see the majestic Dart sweeping first this way, then that, as it makes a giant, sideways-turned S in the area we are about to explore.

This is an easy walk, apart from the first mile, and there is some road walking, later, where you will need to be on your mettle for those turbo-charged speedsters that may be around. Incidentally, several car commercials have been filmed along the road near Poundsgate.

At New Bridge the signpost points to Hannaford. This is a narrow lane that we will follow. In its first few hundred yards it's gentle enough. On the left is a Nature Reserve managed by the Devon Wildlife Trust, the sign stating that it's 'A piece of Devon forever'. When we strolled by, following days of heavy rain, the pond and its surrounds all looked extremely wet and the feeder stream was keeping it nicely topped up.

Stay with the road as it now starts its long climb upwards, the good news being that you won't require crampons or any other mountaineering equipment – a few Dextrose tablets will suffice.

Hannaford, a good old Devonshire name, is regularly spotted along this quiet and pleasant thoroughfare: first in Hannaford Cottage and Lower Hannaford

Farm and a little later in Hannaford Manor (designed by Sir Edwin Lutyens before he started work on Castle Drogo) and Higher Hannaford. Hannaford was once the seat of Sir Robert Torrens. Keep a look out for the stand of palm trees – there's not many of *them* on Dartmoor!

Now the lane gets steeper but after a while the hedge on your left gives way to open moorland. As soon as this happens, leave the road and immediately you will encounter a grassy area. A sign tells you that vehicles can go no farther. Going straight on up the hillside is a green, grassy-looking track. Follow it up and you will notice that ahead is a disused quarry – was it Hannaford Quarry?

Head towards the quarry but climb up the steepish slope on its left-hand side. It's marked by the poles that once linked a fence to keep out the fauna. Carry on up the slope, feeling how well your leg muscles are being toned up, until you reach a clearly defined track that rises from your right and climbs the slope to your left. Turn left onto it and soon you will enjoy the visual delights that this wondrous track offers the walker. Away to your left are some of southern Dartmoor's highest moors, Holne Moor occupying its share of the view.

This track is known as Dr Blackall's Drive. However, it really ought to be called Mrs Blackall's Drive, as her husband had it created for her enjoyment of Dartmoor. Dr Blackall bought Spitchwick Manor in 1867, but when his wife became physically incapable of walking the moors this carriageway became the solution, their pony and trap being a regular sight on fine days. What a drive it is, too, curving around the highest slopes of the Dart Gorge.

Follow it as you spot first the romantic Bench Tor on the far side of the gorge, then the triangular mass of Sharp Tor; last, but not least, Mel Tor on our side of the valley comes into view. Hundreds of feet below, the Dart roars down its canyon; all in all, it must be one of the most strikingly beautiful scenes in Devon. The only let-down is the lack of a tor at Aish Tor!

But we can't get too carried away with the splendour of it all, as there is a special little pub awaiting us: one that can only be reached by some road walking, a small price to pay.

When a wall appears on your right, at a point called Brake Corner, signalling the end of open moorland on one side, turn right to follow it. By keeping it on your left you will eventually reach the road near to the pub. First notice, in the distance, Leusdon Church, which once boasted the oldest vicar in the country and was a place where the late Sir Michael Hordern, grew up and worshipped.

Farther on, the view ahead embraces such landmarks as Buckland Beacon, to the left; Ausewell Woods; and, many miles beyond, a wood-capped hill that is Denbury Hill. Almost in line with this, but on the far horizon, it's possible to pick out the two churches, one with a tower, the other with a spire, at St Marychurch in Torquay. The masts at Westerland, near Marldon, are also visible in clear conditions.

On reaching the road, turn left, and take care to face oncoming traffic. This section is for several hundred yards, so single file is essential. On reaching the Tavistock Inn (01364 631251), at Poundsgate, slow your walking pace down to under 30 mph!

The inn is very old and has all the appearances and features of a farmhouse. In the winter it is a warm and cosy place to visit, with its fires aglow, and in the summer the beer garden has won prizes for its floral splendour … The only note of caution that we would offer is to inspect the other customers for any sign of a cloven hoof: it's believed that the Devil himself has been known to quaff the odd tankard of ale on his visits there, the last being in October 1638.

On leaving the inn, turn left onto the road. A short way along on your left is the Old Post Office, a picturesque cottage, complete with churn. Not far along, a small stream trickles under the road. Here we leave this transmoor route for pastures green. The signpost points to 'Lower Town & Townswood Cottages', and for a few hundred yards it takes us along the side of a field beside the smallest of leats.

At the end we reach a surfaced drive, where we turn right to soon reach a sign pointing left to Spitchwick Farm. Head this way, gently downhill, until the road veers left but you continue straight on! Ahead, on the distant hill, is Buckland Beacon, home of the Ten Commandments, and there you go walking along the edge of the fields staying on the straight and narrow! To your left on the hill is Leusdon's St John the Baptist Church, built in 1863.

Follow the line through these green and pleasant fields, where you might be forgiven for forgetting that this is Dartmoor, the landscape not seeming as wild as that found at higher altitudes. The route drops down to an oasis on your left in the shape of a tree-bordered pond. Just beyond, the path leaves the open fields to plunge into a woodland

corridor, Great Wood, that follows the small stream that issues from the pond and follows, closely, the law of gravity to plunge downwards to the Dart. This downhill romp is pleasant; it that helps to make up for the hundreds of feet climbed in the first mile of the walk. Civilisation appears in the shape of some buildings as yet another gate has to be passed through, onto a road by a diminutive granite bridge. Bear right and continue the downward trend. On the left are the sort of attractive cottages that many stressed-out city folks would love to live in.

Our little stream now leaves us but you can rest assured that it reaches its goal, the mighty Dart, to add its crystal clear waters to its bigger relation's. The road runs down to meet another small one. Turn right, where you might be curious about yellow lines and parking restrictions in so obviously a narrow lane. Well, people will park anywhere if they are not expressly forbidden to do so, and there are some pleasant meadows by the Dart. The parking restrictions run from the beginning of March to the end of October. The road passes the entrance to Spitchwick Manor, complete with its pair of matching lodges.

The road beside the Dart will only need to be followed for a short distance, as it's possible, and highly desirable, to leave the road on the left to walk along some of those flat meadows beside the river, a popular spot in the summer for those whose seaside is 'Spitchwick on Sea,' if you know what we mean! That doesn't detract from the pleasantness of the scene. Head along the valley floor in the general direction of New Bridge, the river being on your left-hand side. The Dart's stream has been braided but its main flow isn't far away; it does its best to cut into the hillside, forming steep bluffs in places. The bit we are walking along is referred to as Deeper Marsh and, like all good things, comes to an end in a bluff on our side of the river. Climb up, as if to reach the road, but don't go onto it: there is a path all the way back to our starting point at New

Bridge. It hogs the river bank, drops down off the bluff and follows a flat course back to New Bridge. Those charged with the cause of ensuring our safety have wisely taken the path to go *under* New Bridge, saving us the need to cross the busy road at this point. The path thus terminates back at the car park that we left a few hours earlier. Go and have an ice cream!

— Walk 6 —
In The Footsteps of Sir Francis
The Skylark Inn, Clearbrook
(about 4 miles)

As we are based in Exeter, in East Devon, we don't get to walk on the far western side of Dartmoor very often, so it was something of a treat to do this short pub stroll on, and below, just one part of Roborough Down. However, for Plymothians it may not seem anything too special for this great open space has long been regarded as a 'back garden' for them, particularly at weekends, when the weather is fine, and hundreds of families utilise the open spaces where public access is permitted.

The starting place, away from the more populated part of the down, is a moderately sized car park just off the main road that runs from Yelverton down to the village of Roborough. It is just yards from the turn-off for the small village of Clearbrook, and just over two miles from Yelverton. The map should help you to locate it but if you want a grid reference, then 509646 should rubber-stamp its whereabouts.

Once you have donned the necessary gear, leave the car park by the way that you drove into it. At the exit you will see on the far side of the road a green track, a pleasant, slightly downhill corridor to help you get into the swing of things. Hoofmarks are evidence of horse riders, or at least the horses!

As you walk along this easy opening stretch, you may notice glimpses to your right of a stone-lined trough. Today it looks like an insignificant enough depression, but it has an interesting history. The name of this former waterway is Drake's Leat, also referred to, and named on the 1907 OS map, as the Plymouth Leat. It was the work of that great Elizabethan sea-dog Sir Francis Drake. It was about Christmas time in 1590 when Drake cut the first sod of this channel that was engineered to carry a plenteous supply of fresh water to a Plymouth that had already 'tapped' most of the freely accessible sources available. It was completed late in the following April and ran for some 18 miles, from the River Mew (or Meavy), below Sheeps Tor, around the hillsides whilst wending its way Plymouthwards.

It was said that, before the leat was constructed, Plymouth was in such dire straights for water that there wasn't enough to wash clothes and that they had to be sent to Plympton to be washed. Legend has it that when the water flowed into it for the first time, Drake escorted the supply all the way down to Plymouth, riding ahead of it on horseback. This watercourse gave good service for about two centuries, but a better, more reliable flow was created by the building of the Devonport Leat in the late eighteenth century, and even this was superseded by Burrator Reservoir, at the end of the nineteenth. These were all measures to satisfy the ever-growing demand of Plymouth.

The course of the Devonport Leat ran almost parallel to this one, and was only yards away, on this part of Roborough Down. It ran at a slightly higher level just to the west of here, and did not follow such elaborate twists as the earlier Drake's Leat.

The first part of Drake's Leat lies submerged at the bottom of the reservoir, thus making it the only bit to have water in it these days! Don't be tempted to walk in the dry bed: it's a favourite with adders so you might get more than you bargained for! Stay on the easier open path and enjoy the view over Dartmoor, the village of Shaugh Prior nestling in the uplands to your right with the great bulk of Shell Top also visible.

So with the leat to your right, the history lesson over for the time being, and the road

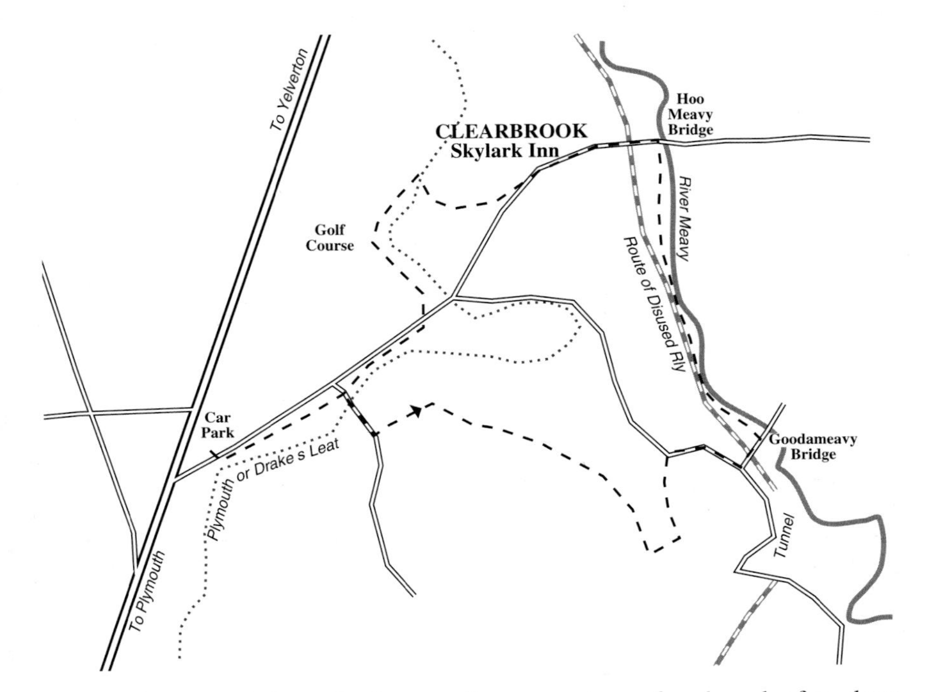

to Clearbrook to your left, walk along until you meet a surfaced road, after about a quarter of a mile. Turn right to cross Drake's Leat in a civilised fashion. Walk a short way along this road until you see a cattle grid that marks the end of the open down and the beginning of enclosed fields. From here to the left a wall runs downhill. Follow the wall, for this perimeter is to be your rough guide for the next half mile or more. A close look at a current OS map will show you that this is the border of the national park; you are still on Dartmoor, but only just. Perhaps someone, some day, will have the idea of introducing a perambulation of this man-made boundary. What a mammoth walk it would be! Well, you can experience part of it as you follow the wall through a gate, followed by a sharp change of direction as it bends right. The track heads straight whilst the wall disappears off for a while before re-emerging a little farther on.

We noticed that swaling had taken place here, this being a deliberate act of setting fire to heathland in order to improve the general growth of grass that will spring up afterwards. The practice, in the past, was traditionally carried out by those who had the rights to graze animals and was usually done in March or April, depending on the harshness of the winter. It is said that this doesn't have a devastating effect on the indigenous wildlife, so you won't stumble over the remains of fried lizards or part-cremated creepy-crawlies. The commoners' rights for grazing on the down covered a range of creatures that included pigs, ponies, geese, donkeys, sheep and cattle.

Head on with the wall to your right, for several hundred yards, wending your way past various waif-like trees until you finally emerge, near a gateway, onto a firm, well-made gravel track. Turn left here and follow the track. Walking beside it will be easier on the old pins, for the grass gives, making for a more comfortable passage. This track turns a fairly sharp bend to the left and then is joined by another from the right. Head straight on for a few yards before turning another bend. The track ahead now changes hue, from a depressing dull colour to a much more cheerful lighter shade. It also starts to drop steeply downwards. Towards the bottom it veers left, but you head straight down to join a metalled road. Cross the cattle grid – or use the gate beside it, if you have poor sight and incredibly small feet.

The downward hill is now even steeper; there are those who find this harder work than going uphill, for there is a certain effort involved in combating the natural increased momentum brought on by the force of gravity. You might regret jogging down the steepest section!

The hill eventually bottoms out and a T-junction is met with a left turn, beneath the old railway bridge, to Goodameavy. Don't be alarmed if you weigh more than 17 tons; you will not have to test the weight capability of Goodameavy Bridge ahead over the Meavy. For your convenience a footpath (not for cyclists!) heads off to the left.

The scenery has now changed from open common to a green and pleasant vale, that of the River Meavy. The next half a mile is generally flat, beside the part-wooded river that tumbles on ever downwards. The disused railway track that runs parallel with you, but on a higher level, to your left, is a line that ran from Marsh Mills, on the outskirts of Plymouth, up the wooded Plym Valley to then follow the Meavy up to Yelverton and beyond. The railway, shown on the 1907 OS map as the 'Launceston Branch', closed in 1962 and two years later the lines were lifted. Today the line is a favourite thoroughfare for cyclists.

For a few hundred yards the meadows are flat, but the path reaches a stile with no style! Cross it to pass a few trees, on a slight rise, to another dry leat. For a short distance this is to your left whilst the river is still to your right. The end of your claustrophobia is attained very quickly, for the path opens out into an even broader and more pleasant flat riverside meadow. Climb a better stile to walk beside the river. Not far ahead there is a little mound with a tree growing out of it. From here you will see the stone structure of Hoo Meavy Bridge ahead. A small ladder enables access to the road.

Look at the first gnarled tree on your right – imagine seeing *that* loom out of the mist on a dank, dark foggy day.

Although a footpath goes on beside the Meavy, the temptation of refreshment at a pub is too much, so the road, to the left, becomes the preferred option. As usual the speed restriction signs indicate that you must slow your walking pace down to less than 30 mph – not that the next section is conducive to a mile every two minutes. There is nothing, to help raise an even greater thirst, like a good bit of healthy uphill walking. (In passing, bearing in mind this is Clearbrook, you might notice that one of the houses here is named Misty Waters.) Pass beneath the old railway bridge and just keep going on uphill until, after some 400 yards, you reach the Skylark Inn (01822 853258) on your right-hand side in another part of Clearbrook. It's likely that this cottage became an inn sometime around the early nineteenth century, when thirsty miners from the nearby Yeoland Consuls mine needed a handily located alehouse. It has been recorded that this pit produced some 475 tons of black tin in the second half of the nineteenth century. What a mine of information!

Having been well fed and watered, leave the inn and turn right to walk along in front of the buildings that line the road. At the end of the buildings turn right onto the open common; a two-slabbed little bridge points the way as you will walk uphill, keeping the wooded stone wall to your right. A low bench is on offer but, unless you have overindulged, it's come too soon to be of any use. Proceed up the slope, but where the wall veers right let it do so, for you continue straight ahead and in about 70 yards you will reach Drake's Leat once more. Should you want a picture of this stone-lined historic waterway, this spot would be the best section that is seen on today's outing.

Cross the leat, and in some 30 yards a disused tramway will be encountered. Although industrial archaeology sounds pretty boring, many people find old mines, quarries, canals and railroads totally absorbing and have the ability to picture what they must have been like in their heyday. It's not difficult to imagine horses pulling wagons of stone. This line, opened on 26 September 1823, ran from the many granite quarries near Princetown for some 25 miles down and off the moor. We turn sharp left onto this old line, where you will see some granite setts still in place, this area once being referred to as North Wharf. When the line opened it was with much joy and celebration and close to this point an enormous marquee was erected to cater for the thousand guests who had been invited to attend for a Big Breakfast, nineteenth-century fashion. Again the going is easy as Yelverton's golf course is skirted.

The line loops around to an isolated building. This was 'Tyrwhitt's Wharf', named after the man who was responsible for much of the development of the area in and

around Princetown, a man of immense vision and incredible optimism. This was where the horses, which plied the line hauling the wagons, were stabled and where their needs were catered for. Pass just to the left of the building, which is now boarded up. Perhaps more importantly, you should head to the left of the elevated tee of the ninth hole so as not to disturb budding Nick Faldos.

The road is nearby, but you will probably have spotted the odd passing car. Cross the road and head over the rough vegetation for about 40 or 50 yards until you meet a path – almost any path. There must be a few rookie golfers, for some fifty yards on the wrong side of the road from the golf course we retrieved a ball in the bracken; so always be wary of badly hooked shots on days when the wind might be blowing strongly from the north west!

Turn right and make your way along the corridor between Drake's Leat, that we meet yet again, and the road. You should soon recognise the green track that you walked down earlier in the walk, which is met on crossing the next road a few hundred yards ahead of you. The rest is (dare we tempt fate?) a doddle, and – hopefully – you will soon spot your car ahead of you up the long gradual slope that leads back to it. A lovely little walk of about four miles. What a way to end a book!